GLOUCESTER
TO
CARDIFF

Vic Mitchell and Keith Smith

MP Middleton Press

Cover Picture: Bound for Severn Tunnel Junction on 6th November 1958, 0-6-0PT no. 7723 stands at Lydney Junction down platform. It will shortly rumble over the crossing of the Lydney Docks branch. (R.S.Carpenter)

Published October 2005

ISBN 1 904474 66 7

© Middleton Press, 2005

Design Emily Pede

Published by
            Middleton Press
            Easebourne Lane
            Midhurst, West Sussex
            GU29 9AZ
Tel: 01730 813169
Fax: 01730 812601
Email: info@middletonpress.co.uk
www.middletonpress.co.uk

Printed & bound by Biddles Ltd, Kings Lynn

INDEX

ACKNOWLEDGEMENTS

We are very grateful for the assistance from many of those mentioned in the credits also to C.L.Caddy, A.R.Carder, R.Caston, R.A.Cooke, L.Crosier, G.Croughton, J.H.Day, D.Edge, T.J.Edgington, N.Langridge, B.W.Leslie, M.Oakley, Mr D. and Dr S.Salter, E.Wilmshurst and particularly our ever supportive wives, Barbara Mitchell and Janet Smith.

I.   Railway Clearing House map of 1947.

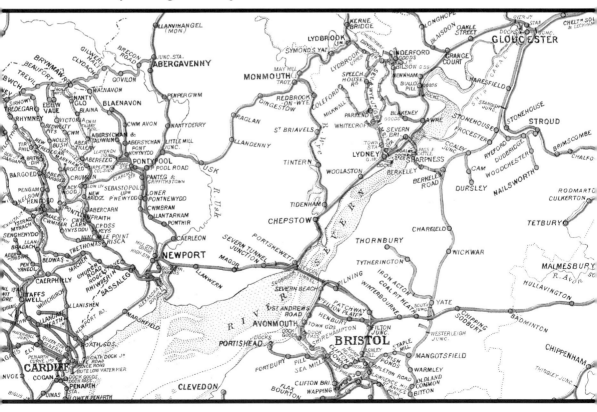

GEOGRAPHICAL SETTING

A trading centre since at least Roman times, Gloucester was the lowest crossing point of the River Severn by road until 1966 and by rail until 1879 when a bridge was completed near Lydney.

The route to Cardiff is along the relatively flat northern flank of the River Severn and its estuary. The line traverses mostly Marl, but in the Newnham - Chepstow area it cuts through or runs across outcrops of Limestone and Sandstone. The same applies in the vicinity of Newport, where a major port developed at the confluence of the River Usk and the Ebbw River. A smaller port had once thrived at the mouth of the River Wye, at Chepstow. This valley is deeply incised and presented a major bridging problem. Limestone was quarried in this vicinity and generated substantial rail traffic.

The other great port on our journey grew between the mouths of the River Taff and Rhymney River at Cardiff. This became a city a century ago and, more recently, the administrative centre of Wales.

The national boundary was on the eastern border of Cardiff until 1974, when Monmouthshire became part of Wales and the border became the River Wye.

The maps are to the scale of 25ins to 1 mile, with north at the top, unless otherwise indicated.

II.   Gradient Profile. The mileage on the left part is from London via Gloucester, while that on the right is via the Severn Tunnel.

HISTORICAL BACKGROUND

The first passenger railway to Gloucester was that of the Birmingham & Gloucester Railway which opened in 1840. Next was the Bristol & Gloucester Railway in 1844. Both became part of the Midland Railway in 1845, the year which the line from Swindon was completed. This was broad gauge and was operated by the Great Western Railway.

The South Wales Railway was also broad gauge and opened between Chepstow, Cardiff and Swansea on 19th June 1850. The Gloucester to Chepstow section came into use on 19th September 1851, but through running was not possible until 19th July 1852, when the bridge over the River Wye was completed. The SWR was also operated by the GWR from the outset.

There was an earlier line at Cardiff, this being the standard gauge Taff Vale Railway of 1840, which terminated at Cardiff Docks.

The SWR became part of the GWR in 1863 and the route was converted to standard gauge in 1872. The associated lines are listed in geographical order, together with the passenger operation dates. Goods dates and freight-only branches are included in the captions.

To Ledbury 1885 to 1959
To Hereford 1855 to 1964
To Cinderford 1854 to 1958
To Sharpness 1879 to 1960
To Whitecroft 1869 to 1929
To Monmouth 1876 to 1959
To Severn Tunnel 1886 to date
To Hereford via Caerleon 1874 to date
To Pontypool direct 1852 to 1880
To Risca 1855 to 1962
To Bargoed 1865 to 1962

A service was maintained on the Whitecroft line as far as Lydney Town until 1960. It ceased when the Severn Bridge was damaged and the Sharpness service was withdrawn.

Upon nationalisation in 1948, the route became part of the Western Region of British Railways. Privatisation in 1996 resulted in South Wales & West providing services ("South" was dropped in 1998). However, after reorganisation in 2001, Wales & Borders became the franchisee. Arriva Trains Wales took over in December 2003. Other services were provided by Central Trains, a name unchanged since 1996. Two other companies operated through the Severn Tunnel and on to Cardiff; in 2005 they were First Great Western and Wessex Trains.

PASSENGER SERVICES

The first through service comprised five weekday and three Sunday trains.

The timetable for 1869 weekdays showed four fast trains and four slow, plus two starting at Chepstow. On Sundays the figures were two, one and one.

In 1885 the pattern of weekday through services was similar, but there was an additional train starting at Portskewett at 7.0am. It ran at 10.0am on Sundays, along with a stopping train from Gloucester and one from Chepstow.

The opening of the Severn Tunnel did not affect the number of trains between Gloucester and South Wales. Only the eastern section of the route will be considered herein, as the part westward is discussed in *Swindon to Newport*.

By 1907, there were five stopping trains and five fast; Sundays - one and three. There were also several short workings. Twenty years later, the numbers were five and ten on weekdays with one and two on Sundays.

World War II brought a reduction in fast trains, this continuing in the following austerity years. However, the Sunday service improved, with 1947 having five trains, although two were at night.

In 1964, daytime weekday trains stopping at all stations numbered seven; five more started at Chepstow and there were six long distance services, with four of them on Sundays.

With full dieselisation by 1967, the number of departures from Gloucester on weekdays was 13, with 8 on Sundays. There was also one from Chepstow on weekday mornings; this was still running in 1988, by which time there were also two in the afternoon. The through service was basically hourly, with fewer on Sundays.

The daily pattern in 2004 was an hourly fast train, with a stopping one between most of them. This provided the best service ever on the route.

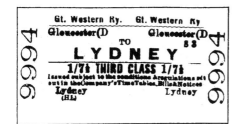

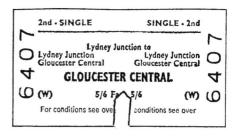

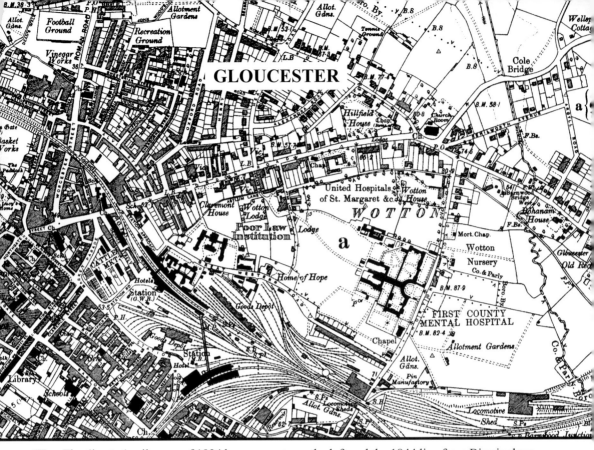

III.   The 6ins to 1 mile map of 1924 has our route on the left and the 1844 line from Birmingham on the right. Its terminus was east of the South Wales Railway station of 1851, which is left of centre. The complex alterations to the tracks south and east thereof are outside the scope of this volume and are shown in diagrams in our *Gloucester to Bristol* album. The ex-SWR station was named "Central" from 17th September 1951; the curved platforms below it became "Eastgate" on tht day. The suffixes were dropped on 26th May 1968 and the latter station was closed on 1st December 1975.

(lower left) 1. This station was used by the GWR, the Midland Railway running through the other. The map shows them to be connected by a long footbridge. There are crossovers at both platforms, allowing four through trains to load simultaneously. The staff here numbered 233 in 1923. (Lens of Sutton coll.)

2.   At the west end of the down platform, a train for Hereford stands in the bay, alongside the line for the loading dock. The train is the 6.20pm on 8th May 1948. On the skyline is Middle Box; it had a 51-lever frame and closed in about 1938. (R.G.Nelson/T.Walsh)

3.   BR class 9F 2-10-0 no. 92243 was recorded on the up through line on 29th August 1964 with a train of coke wagons. The other locomotive is on the bridge over London Road. (G.Adams/M.J.Stretton)

4.   The train from Cardiff to Leeds bends over London Road as no. D7033 passes West Box on 22nd August 1964. The box had 22 levers and closed on 26th May 1968. In the bay is 2-6-2T no. 4107. (R.E.Toop)

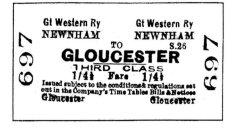

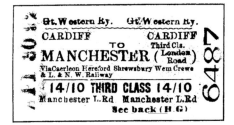

5.   The elegant GWR structure was destroyed and replaced by this featureless block in 1977. It is seen soon after completion. It required complete re-roofing in 2004. (D.Thompson)

6.   The former up platform was used for parcels only from 1968 and is obscured by parcels vans in this 1977 view. The station originally had only one long platform on the south side, a common GWR practice in its early years. (H.C.Casserley)

7.	This is the west end in July 1977 with a stopping train for Cardiff in the bay. The platform on the left was used for passengers again from 1984. A new footbridge had to be built, as its predecessor had been dismantled in the 1960s. (D.Thompson)

8.	A class 153 single DMU arrives from Cardiff to form the 10.50 departure from platform 3 on 9th July 2005. Adequate weather protection was provided at this end of platform 2, unlike its eastern extension. (V.Mitchell)

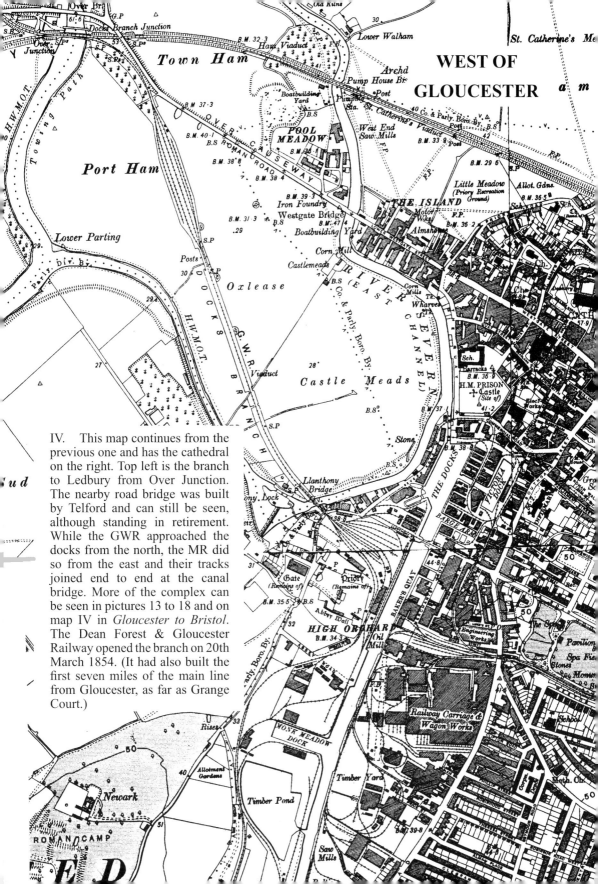

WEST OF GLOUCESTER

IV.   This map continues from the previous one and has the cathedral on the right. Top left is the branch to Ledbury from Over Junction. The nearby road bridge was built by Telford and can still be seen, although standing in retirement. While the GWR approached the docks from the north, the MR did so from the east and their tracks joined end to end at the canal bridge. More of the complex can be seen in pictures 13 to 18 and on map IV in *Gloucester to Bristol*. The Dean Forest & Gloucester Railway opened the branch on 20th March 1854. (It had also built the first seven miles of the main line from Gloucester, as far as Grange Court.)

9.   The docks branch is on the left of this 1959 westward panorama and Over Junction is in the distance. The Ledbury branch curves right near the signal box, which was in use to 2nd June 1969. The branch closed in 1964; it is featured in our *Worcester to Hereford* album. (P.J.Garland/R.S.Carpenter)

10.   The bridge girders span the River Severn, Docks Junction being just visible beyond them. Part of Telford's bridge and the Ledbury line can be seen behind the signal box, which was opened by 1885. It was extended in 1903 to take a 53-lever frame. The box seen was replaced in January 1953 by a non-standard brick box with a 58-lever frame, which closed in June 1969. Parts of the two goods loops are in the foreground. They could each accommodate two trains and Over Sidings signal box of 1904 was part way along them until closed in 1969. The loops had been extended west in 1942, when three sidings were added on the north side for wartime traffic. (British Railways)

GLOUCESTER DOCKS

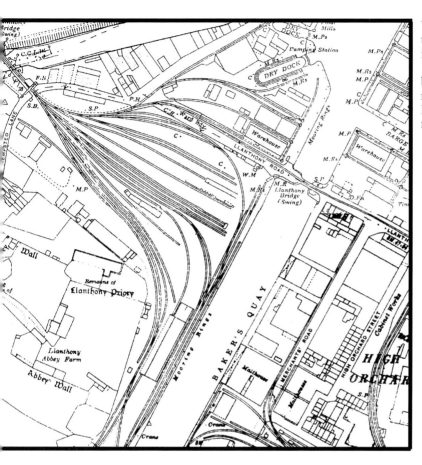

V. The LMS part of the dock lines is shown in more detail on the 1936 extract. Two swing bridges are included; the right one was the LMS limit. The scale has been reduced slightly.

11. Llanthony Sidings are in the background as 2-6-0 no. 78005 pushes its train towards Docks Branch Junction. It will use the crossover at Over Junction, before running east. On the left is the A40. (M.A.N.Johnston)

12.   The Dock Branch served the 1941 Castle Meads Power Station, which supplied steam for its fireless Barclay 0-4-0, seen in about 1965. It was in use until 1969. Castle Meads is in the middle of . The branch was mixed gauge from 1869 and standard only from 1872. (S.Apperley/ C.G.Maggs)

13.   Llanthony Yard was in terminal decline when a Branch Line Society tour visited it on 3rd April 1982. The line in the right background curves south to run close to the Gloucester & Berkeley Canal. Branch closure was in 1989. (D.H.Mitchell)

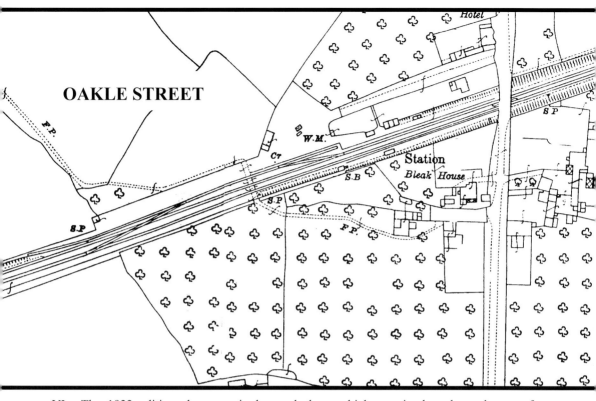

OAKLE STREET

VI. The 1922 edition shows a single goods loop which remained unchanged, apart from lengthening in the 1870s. The station opened with the route, but was closed from 1856 until 1870.

14. This postcard includes the signal box (closed on 21st March 1953 and replaced by a ground frame released from Grange Court signalbox, to access the goods yard), the modest buildings and a massive urinal. The staff of six in 1903 had dropped to four in 1935. (Lens of Sutton coll.)

15.   The 12.35pm Gloucester to Hereford calls on 1st June 1964. The goods yard closed on 12th August 1963 and had been lifted. Passenger service ceased on 2nd November 1964. Orchards abound in this vicinity. (R.G.Nelson/T.Walsh)

Oakle Street	1903	1913	1923	1933
Passenger tickets issued	9417	8885	3197	1887
Season tickets issued	*	*	59	13
Parcels forwarded	3002	4101	3286	3572
General goods forwarded (tons)	749	1223	311	51
Coal and coke received (tons)22	65	28	8	
Other minerals received (tons)	586	2184	2690	398
General goods received (tons)	289	358	487	168
Trucks of livestock handled	1020	1668	1879	426

(* not available.)

GRANGE COURT

16.   Two fascinating photographs from 1872 show gauge conversion in progress. This is probably the last broad gauge train and is serving the vast army of labourers required for the task. Crossbar signals seem ideal posing points. (C.G.Maggs coll.)

17.   Hollow bridge rails were secured to longitudinal timbers which were spaced by transoms, thus the effort required was much greater than sliding one rail across the sleepers. It seems that there was originally a signal box on the bridge. (C.G.Maggs coll.)

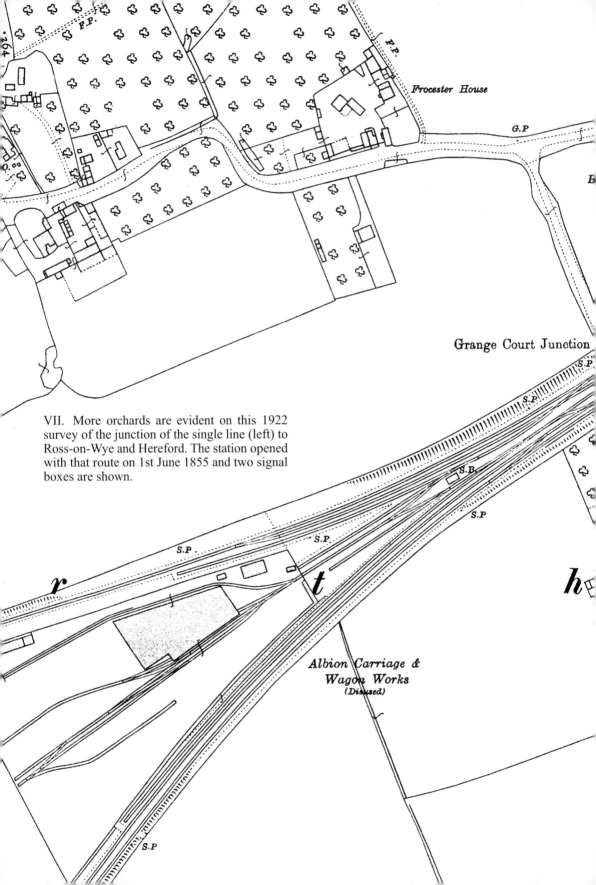

Frocester House

G.P

Grange Court Junction

S.P

S.P

S.B.

S.P

VII. More orchards are evident on this 1922 survey of the junction of the single line (left) to Ross-on-Wye and Hereford. The station opened with that route on 1st June 1855 and two signal boxes are shown.

S.P

S.P

r

t

h

Albion Carriage & Wagon Works
(Disused)

S.P

S.P

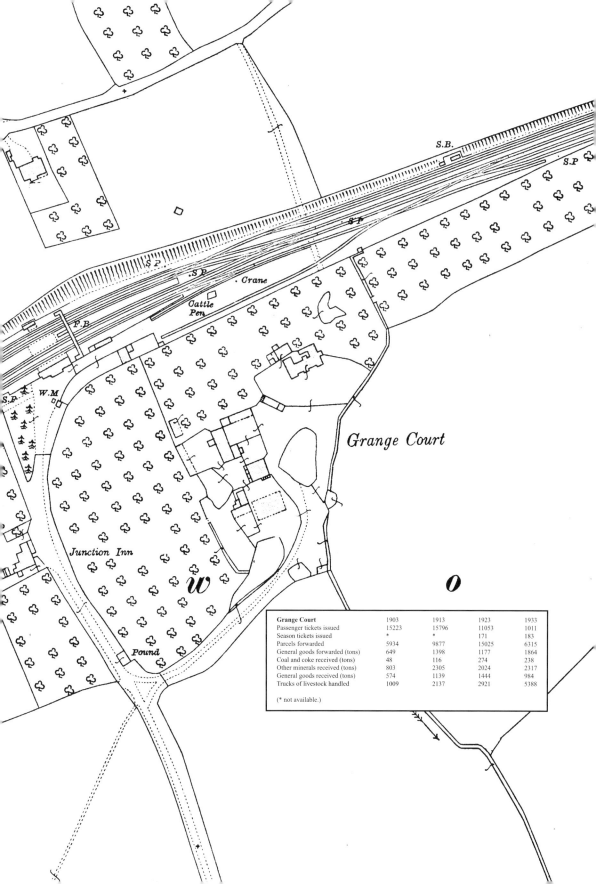

S.B.

S.P

S.P

.S.P

.S.P

Crane

Cattle
Pen

F.B.

S.P

W.M

Grange Court

Junction Inn

w

o

Pound

Grange Court	1903	1913	1923	1933
Passenger tickets issued	15223	15796	11053	1011
Season tickets issued	*	*	171	183
Parcels forwarded	5934	9877	15025	6315
General goods forwarded (tons)	649	1398	1177	1864
Coal and coke received (tons)	48	116	274	238
Other minerals received (tons)	803	2305	2024	2317
General goods received (tons)	574	1139	1444	984
Trucks of livestock handled	1009	2137	2921	5388

(* not available.)

18.   A faded postcard from about 1905 features the platforms which had been greatly lengthened in 1897. The wide space between tracks was due to the broad gauge; the platform could not be repositioned due to the road bridge. (Lens of Sutton coll.)

19.   The main building is on the left, on the south side, and is seen in April 1955 from the cattle dock. There were 16 men employed here in the period 1929-34. (R.M.Casserley)

20.   This signal box replaced the previous two of 1897 on 14th April 1935. It had 68 levers and lasted until 2nd June 1969. No. 6304 is of the 4300 class and is speeding east in about 1962. (R.S.Carpenter)

21.   The Hereford line curves to the right, and to the left of it are the 1901 buildings of the former C&W works. It had various occupants after 1910, including a floor covering manufacturer. Its sidings were in use until 1965, when the Hereford line closed. This photo is from June 1964 and includes the up loop. (R.G.Nelson/T.Walsh)

22.   The 4.18pm Gloucester to Cardiff DMU speeds west on 8th June 1963 and passes the goods yard, which closed three months later. Passenger service ceased here on 2nd November 1964 and little evidence now remains. The up loop was extended to the end of the cutting in 1976, where the down loop ends. Both were rusty in 2005. (R.E.Toop)

WESTBURY-ON-SEVERN HALT

23.   This halt was about 1½ miles from Grange Court and was opened on 9th July 1928. It was photographed in 1958 and closed on 10th August 1959. (Stations UK)

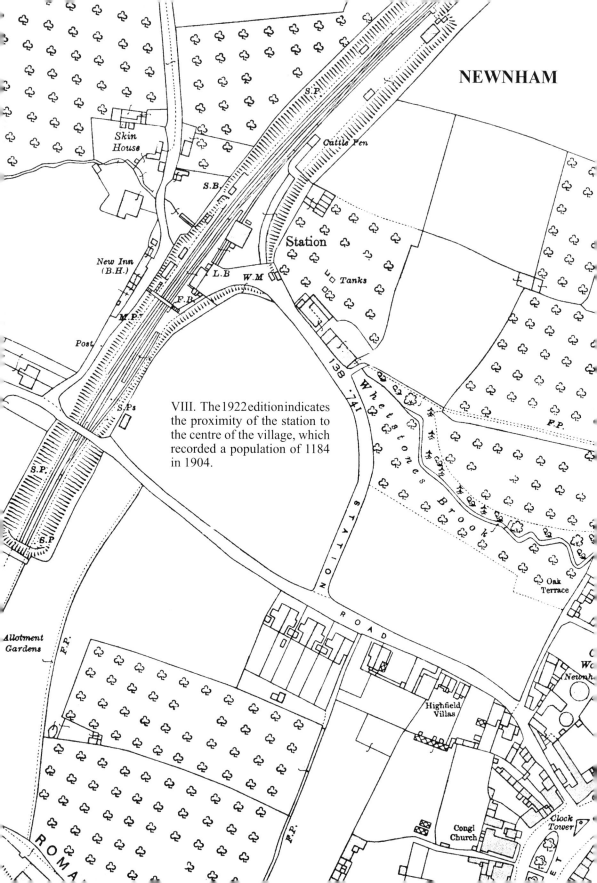

NEWNHAM

VIII. The 1922 edition indicates the proximity of the station to the centre of the village, which recorded a population of 1184 in 1904.

24.   A Gloucester to Newport train is behind 4-4-0 no. 3546 in the 1903-06 period. A bay platform was created on the right on 4th August 1907 and the main line platforms were lengthened at that time. (Lens of Sutton coll.)

Newnham	1903	1913	1923	1933
Passenger tickets issued	29335	46491	33641	17213
Season tickets issued	*	*	282	160
Parcels forwarded	11128	11168	11612	8399
General goods forwarded (tons)	430	746	529	353
Coal and coke received (tons)	342	70	178	19
Other minerals received (tons)	728	2395	655	656
General goods received (tons)	1661	1703	1143	358
Trucks of livestock handled	176	234	135	16

(* not available.)

25.   A view in the other direction includes the high ground on which the village was built, west of the line. Staffing levels dropped from eight in 1903 to four in 1933. (Lens of Sutton coll.)

26.   The bay for Forest of Dean branch trains to Cinderford is evident in this southward view from the footbridge. The branch passenger service ceased on 3rd November 1958, but the bay was not used after 24th March 1957. (J.Moss/R.S.Carpenter)

27. Turning round, we can see part of the goods yard; it closed on 12th August 1963. The signal box (centre) had 20 levers and lasted in use until 24th March 1957. (J.Moss/R.S.Carpenter)

28. The 1.45pm Cardiff General to Cheltenham was recorded on 30th August 1960. Trains ceased to call on 2nd November 1964. (H.B.Priestley/Milepost 92½)

WEST OF NEWNHAM

29.   This is the west end of the 232yd long Newnham Tunnel on 25th April 1982. The HST is working the 10.15 Paddington to Swansea, which had been diverted from the Severn Tunnel, due to engineering work. (T.Heavyside)

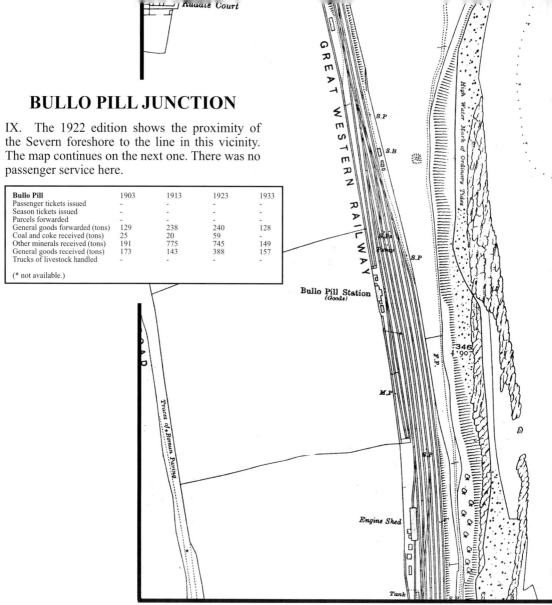

BULLO PILL JUNCTION

IX. The 1922 edition shows the proximity of
the Severn foreshore to the line in this vicinity.
The map continues on the next one. There was no
passenger service here.

Bullo Pill	1903	1913	1923	1933
Passenger tickets issued	-	-	-	-
Season tickets issued	-	-	-	-
Parcels forwarded	-	-	-	-
General goods forwarded (tons)	129	238	240	128
Coal and coke received (tons)	25	20	59	-
Other minerals received (tons)	191	775	745	149
General goods received (tons)	173	143	388	157
Trucks of livestock handled	-	-	-	-

(* not available.)

30. *Rob Roy* was hauling the night
mail from New Milford on 5th
November 1868 when it collided with
a cattle train south of the junction. The
guard and two drovers were killed as
well as cattle. (C.G.Maggs coll.)

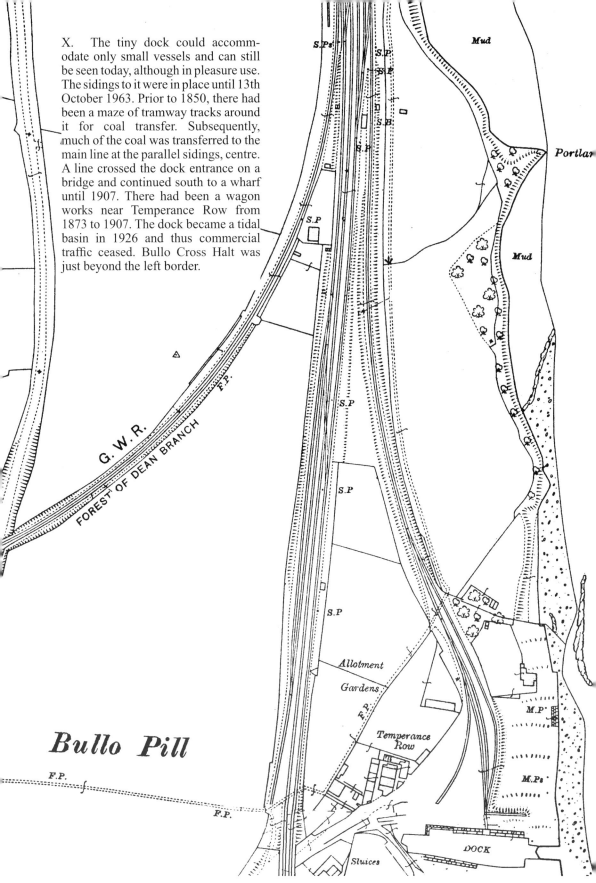

X. The tiny dock could accommodate only small vessels and can still be seen today, although in pleasure use. The sidings to it were in place until 13th October 1963. Prior to 1850, there had been a maze of tramway tracks around it for coal transfer. Subsequently, much of the coal was transferred to the main line at the parallel sidings, centre. A line crossed the dock entrance on a bridge and continued south to a wharf until 1907. There had been a wagon works near Temperance Row from 1873 to 1907. The dock became a tidal basin in 1926 and thus commercial traffic ceased. Bullo Cross Halt was just beyond the left border.

Mud

S.Ps

S.P

S.P

S.B

S.P

Portlar

Mud

S.P

S.P

G. W. R.

FOREST OF DEAN BRANCH

F.P.

S.P

S.P

S.P

Allotment

Gardens

M.P

Bullo Pill

F.P.

F.P.

Temperance Row

M.Ps

DOCK

Sluices

31.   The engine shed is shown on map IX and was in use until 1931, although it was not demolished until 1953. Visible through it is the "Goods Station", which justified a station master. (M.Dart coll.)

32. The 49-lever West Box of 1898 is seen from a train bound for Cinderford on 25th May 1957. The line to Bullo Pill Dock drops away to the left of the ringed signal. The box closed on 18th March 1968. East Box (near the top of map IX) had 20 levers and was in use until 2nd June 1969. A goods loop was added west of it in 1930. (F.Hornby)

33. A photo from 17th May 1965 shows a loaded coal train at the end of the 1 in 54 descent at the end of the branch. The tank on the left was added in 1922; the original one has a small coal stage under it. East Box is in the distance. Ruddle Road Halt was ¼ mile north thereof from 1907 to 1917. (R.K.Blencowe/M.J.Stretton)

AWRE JUNCTION

XI.   This was the junction with the Forest of Dean
Central Railway of 1868, which was broad gauge
until 1872 and became part of the GWR in 1923. The
map is from 1922 and shows two gates across the
single line branch. The station replaced Gatcombe,
which was almost one mile to the south.

Awre Jct	1903	1913	1923	1933
Passenger tickets issued	8083	7537	7712	2695
Season tickets issued	*	*	21	11
Parcels forwarded 8565	12904	15802	10871	
General goods forwarded (tons)	279	266	121	194
Coal and coke received (tons)	277	-	-	-
Other minerals received (tons)	168	311	203	290
General goods received (tons)	304	283	170	175
Trucks of livestock handled	181	185	132	137

(* not available.)

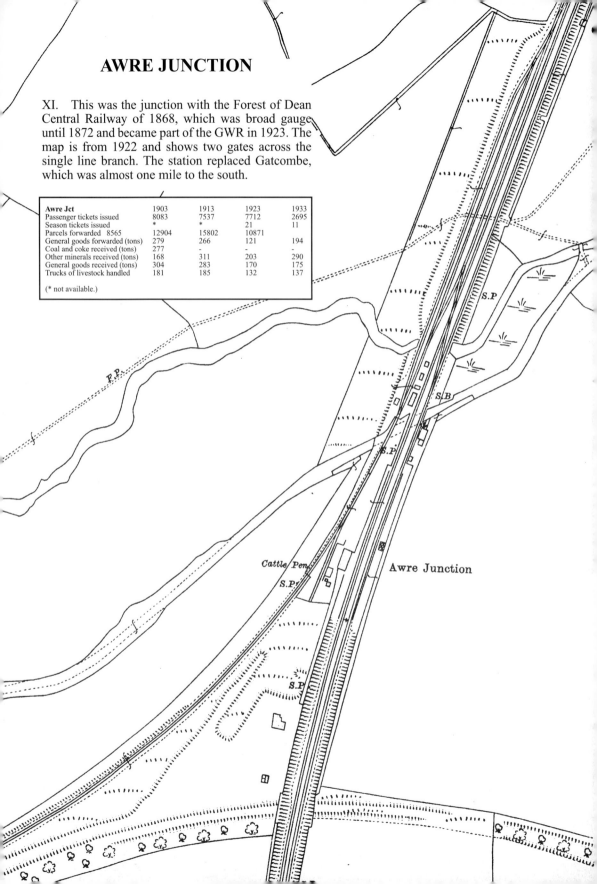

F.P.

S.P.

S.B.

S.P.

Cattle Pen

S.P.

Awre Junction

S.P.

S.P.

34. The GWR station opened on 1st April 1869, its running-in board proclaiming "Awre for Blakeney". The latter had only a goods station. Awre Junction had a staff of six between 1903 and 1938; passenger service was withdrawn on 10th August 1959. (Lens of Sutton coll.)

35. A view north in October 1960 includes a DMU running towards Gloucester and the 1909 signal box, which had a 28-lever frame and functioned as a block post until 2nd June 1969. It controlled the gates until December 1973 and lifting barriers until November 1974. The barriers are now controlled remotely by Lydney box via CCTV, although Awre Junction box remains and can be used to control them in an emergency. (M.A.N.Johnston)

36. Turning round, we see the FoDCR's building and cattle dock. The freight-only branch to Blakeney (right) closed in 1949 (officially 1959), but the section seen was used as a goods yard until 11th September 1961. (M.A.N.Johnston)

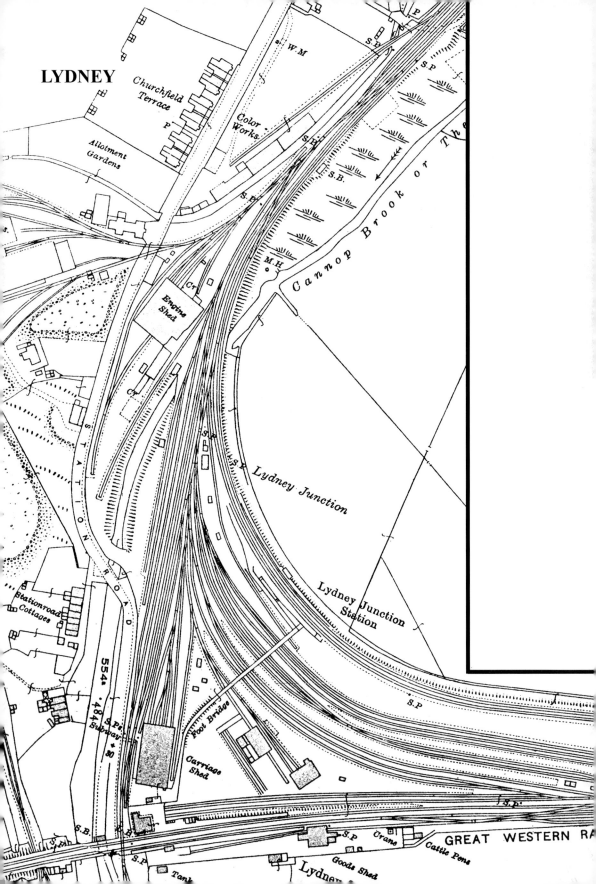

37.   The "baulk road" is evident in this view of the derailment of a broad gauge locomotive close to Lydney station, allegedly. No details survive. (C.G.Maggs coll.)

XII. The 1921 edition has our route across both pages and a footbridge linking both stations. The curved station is that of the Severn & Wye branch of the Midland & GW Joint Railway of 1869. The upper track on the right carried passengers across the Severn to Sharpness and Berkeley Road from 1879 to 1960. The fan of sidings upper left served Lydney Tin Plate Works and its narrow gauge tramway to the docks passes under the main line lower left. Nearby, an S&W track crosses the main line on the level on its way to the docks. The connections between the companies on the right page allowed trains diverted from the Severn Tunnel to use the Severn Bridge. On the right page are two signal boxes: the upper one (centre) was built by the MR in 1914 and was called Otters Pool Junction. The other is the GWR's 84-lever Lydney Junction Box. The former closed in 1965 and the latter in 1969. To the right of the carriage shed are the buildings of Wagon Repairs Ltd. The signal box near the top of the map was named "Lydney Engine Shed" and lasted until 2nd October 1967. Stone trains ran on the branch until 1976.

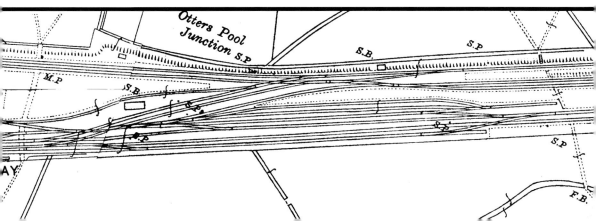

38.   These are the main line platforms, looking west. On the right is the S&W carriage shed, which was built on the site of its terminus, which closed on 16th October 1879. The shed had been in use as a church in Cheltenham until 1880; it was iron clad. The average manning level was 23 in the 1930s. (C.G.Maggs coll.)

Lydney	1903	1913	1923	1933
Passenger tickets issued	24775	29714	37740	29482
Season tickets issued	*	*	171	53
Parcels forwarded	9923	12213	25439	21819
General goods forwarded (tons)	356	514	922	456
Coal and coke received (tons)6	53	62	50	
Other minerals received (tons)	506	295	2598	1032
General goods received (tons)	1325	1779	4922	4710
Trucks of livestock handled	212	188	90	51

(* not available.)

39.   The Brunel chalet-style buildings were recorded in about 1923, with the goods shed in the distance. Goods traffic ceased to be handled on 1st August 1967. Both stations used the suffix "Junction" from 21st May 1955 until 6th May 1968. (Stations UK)

40.   The S&W platforms of 1879 were provided with even more modest buildings. On the right is part of the 1908 footbridge, which passed over no less than 12 curved sidings, a great potential danger on the level. (Stations UK)

41.   The ramps to the bridge were gently inclined to facilitate luggage and parcel transfer. At one period, about 20 milk churns were manhandled daily along this structure. MR signs and fencing are evident, as is the tinplate works, in this 1950 view. (R.S.Carpenter)

42.   The 25-lever West Box controlled the crossing of the road and the track to Lydney Docks. Approaching from Cardiff on 6th November 1958 is 4-6-0 no. 5914 *Ripon Hall*. The docks line closed on 25th August 1963 and the crossing was removed within a month. (R.S.Carpenter)

43.   The S&W engine shed is shown on the left of map XII and is seen in September 1962. Centre is the running shed and left is the repair shop, plus the former coaling dock. Ironically, Forest of Dean coal was unsuitable for locomotives. On the right is the stores, office and sand dryer. The shed closed on 2nd March 1964. (R.S.Carpenter)

44.   The down side retained its original roofline, while the up side had kept part of the earlier platform, when photographed in 1964. (R.G.Nelson/T.Walsh)

45.　We now have two photographs from 9th July 2005. A single class 153 car formed the 10.50 Gloucester to Cardiff service and it is passing the former West Box, which controlled only gates from March 1969 and barriers after February 1972. The down side shelter was similar to the original. (V.Mitchell)

46.　The Dean Forest Railway began restoration work at Norchard in 1974 and, to cut a long story short, created an island platform on the site of the 1879 S&W station, plus a building of the original style. The 11.20 departure was hauled by no. 27006. On the right is one of two recent arrivals from South West Trains; they came over the connection with the up goods loop. The link was deemed unsuitable for use by through passenger charters from the main line. (V.Mitchell)

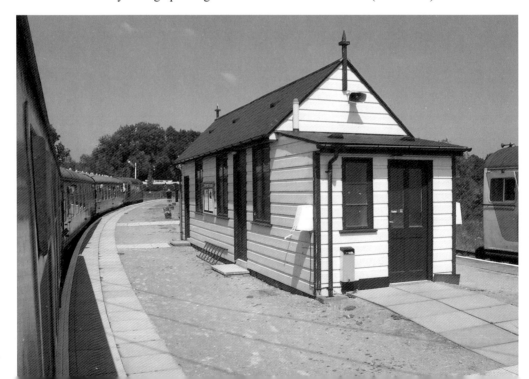

LYDNEY DOCKS

XIII. This map continues from the lower left part of map XII and includes the narrow gauge tramway from Lydney Tinplate Works. The tips on the east bank were scrapped in 1927.

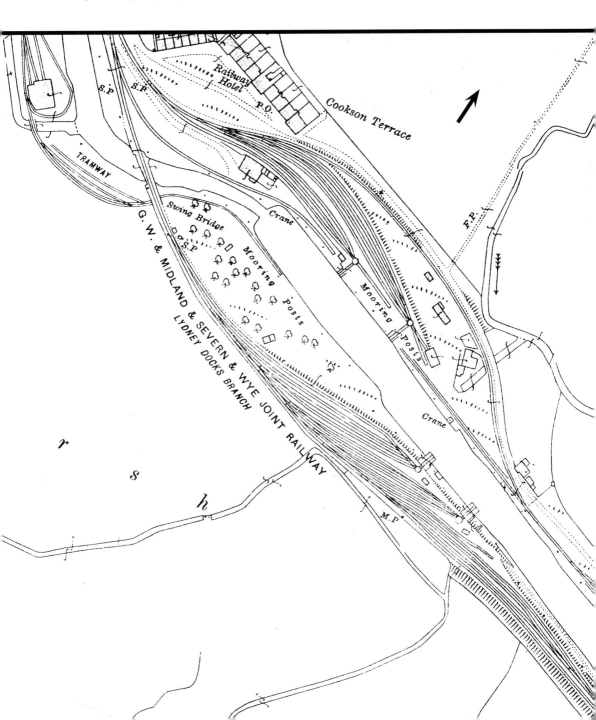

47. This northward view has the S&W offices in the background; it is shown on map XIII. The wagons belong to Parkend Deep Navigation Collieries. (C.G.Maggs coll.)

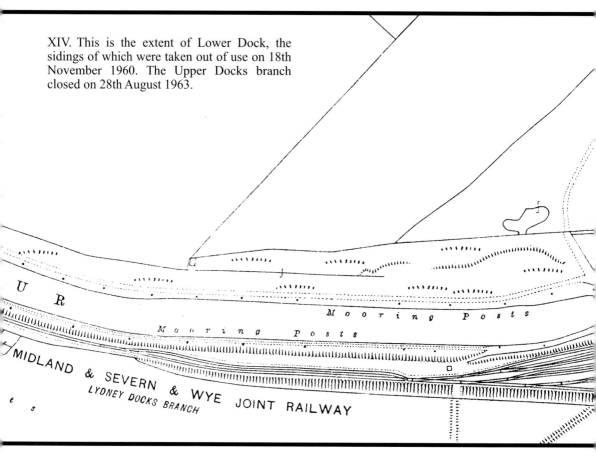

XIV. This is the extent of Lower Dock, the sidings of which were taken out of use on 18th November 1960. The Upper Docks branch closed on 28th August 1963.

48.   The tip winches were operated manually, unlike the hydraulically powered units at the larger docks. A total of nine tips were built. (C.G.Maggs coll.)

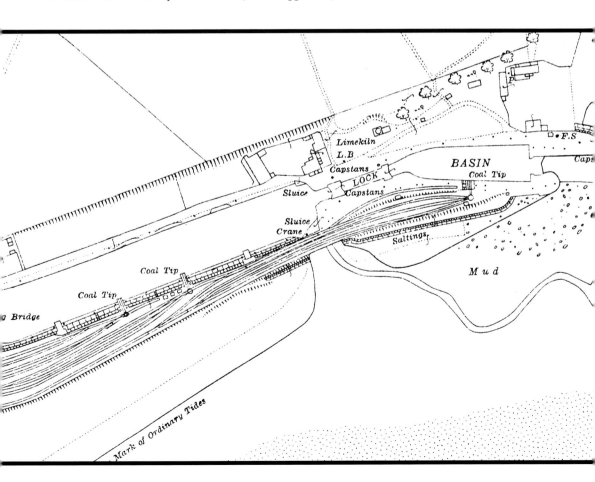

Limekiln
L.B
Capstans
Sluice
LOCK
Capstans
BASIN
Coal Tip
F.S
Cap

Sluice
Crane
Saltings
Mud

Coal Tip
Coal Tip
Bridge
Mark of Ordinary Tides

WOOLASTON

XV.   This isolated station opened on 1st June 1853, but the siding in the woodland did not appear until about 1907.

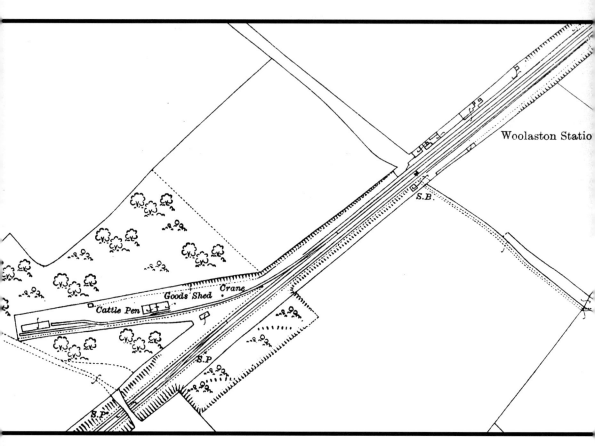

Woolaston Statio

Woolaston	1903	1913	1923	1933
Passenger tickets issued	6192	7312	9500	2113
Season tickets issued	*	*	64	*
Parcels forwarded	3578	6017	9041	3008
General goods forwarded (tons)	813	724	3208	129
Coal and coke received (tons)	46	17	39	18
Other minerals received (tons)	205	386	245	959
General goods received (tons)	1406	1387	946	588
Trucks of livestock handled	53	30	77	26

(* not available.)

49. All service was withdrawn on 1st December 1954 and this view towards Lydney was recorded in 1958. There had been a staff of four or five between the wars. (Stations UK)

50. An up freight passes through on 30th August 1960, hauled by 2-8-0 no. 3837. The signal box was in use from about 1879 until 19th January 1969. The 1916 frame had 17 levers. (H.B.Priestley/ Milepost 92½)

TUTSHILL HALT

XVI. The halt was in use from 9th July 1934 until 5th January 1959 and is shown top right on this 1946 map at 1ins to 1 mile. There was a three-mile long branch south from a point near Tidenham (right) to Beachley Shipyard in 1917-19; it officially closed in January 1928. Built during the next conflict was a branch to a military depot near Caerwent (centre left). This has been added to the map with a solid line.

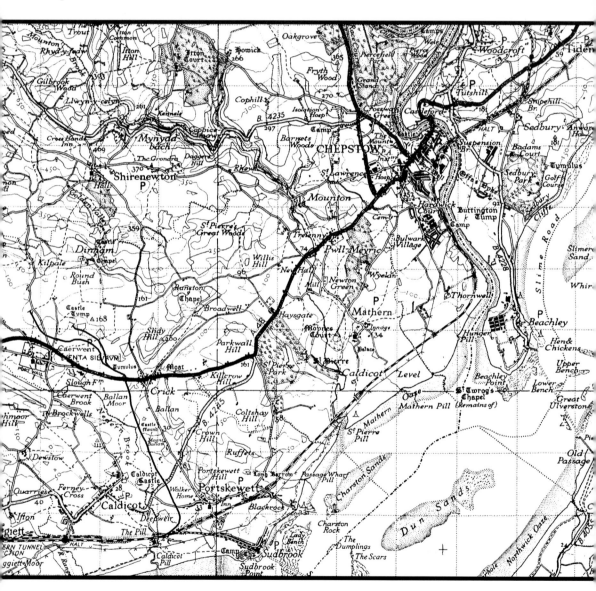

51.   This eastward view is from April 1955 and is from a train bound for Monmouth, using the 1 in 66 incline on the left. There were steep paths up from both platforms. On the right is Wye Valley Junction box, which had a 25-lever frame in use from 1875 to 3rd March 1969. (H.C.Casserley)

EAST OF CHEPSTOW

52.   The tubular suspension bridge was designed by I.K.Brunel to span the River Wye from a limestone cliff on the east bank to 9ft diameter cast iron cylinders, filled with concrete and based on rock 40ft below the river bed. The main tubes were hoisted in place, one end having been floated out on a pontoon. The 460 tons of wrought iron for the trusses were hung under them without the use of scaffolding! The first tube was positioned on 8th April 1852 and the second one was supporting trains from 18th April 1853. The station is on the right; the temporary Chepstow East terminus had been on the left. (C.G.Maggs coll.)

53.   Seen from the cliff on 25th April 1982 is the diverted 12.50 Swansea to Paddington HST, the station footbridge being in the left background. Brunel's bridge was rebuilt with lattice girders in 1962, the headroom for shipping having been wwreduced since the 1850s. The shorter spans had been replaced in 1948. (T.Heavyside)

CHEPSTOW

54.   This engraving was probably made in 1851 to give an impression of the station as a terminus for trains from the west. Staff increased from 14 in 1903 to 33 in 1936. Brunel's stone buildings on both sides of the line were raised 22 inches in order to accommodate the raising of the low platforms, about which there had for long been complaints. The job was carried out between 12th November 1877 and 13th February 1878. Forty-one men and lifting jacks were employed and not a pane of window glass was broken. (C.G.Maggs coll.)

55.   The portal towers supporting the suspension tubes of Chepstow Bridge are evident. Trains were subject to a 15mph speed limit for many years, while running over this structure. This postcard is from about 1905. (Lens of Sutton coll.)

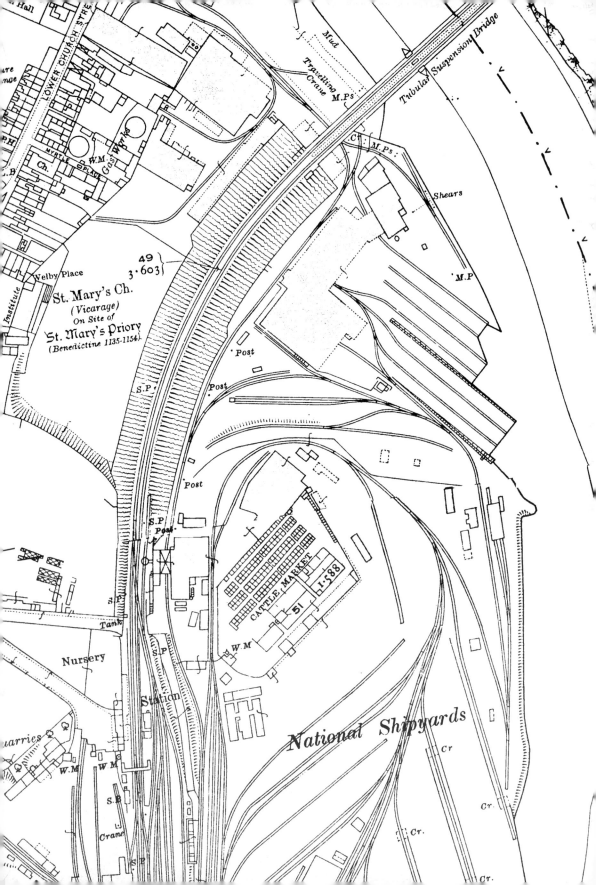

St. Mary's Ch.
(Vicarage)
On Site of
St. Mary's Priory
(Benedictine 1135-1154)

LOWER CHURCH STREET

Welby Place

W.M.

Gas Works

MYRTLE PLACE

Ch.

Hall

Institute

Nursery

Station

Quarries

W.M.

W.M.

Tank

Crane

49
3·603

Post

Post

Post

S.P.

S.P.

S.P.

S.P.

S.P.

S.P.

Post

W.M.

CATTLE MARKET
51
1·588

National Shipyards

Travelling
Crane
M.Ps

Mud

Tubular Suspension Bridge

M.Ps

Shears

M.P

Cr.

Cr.

Cr.

Cr.

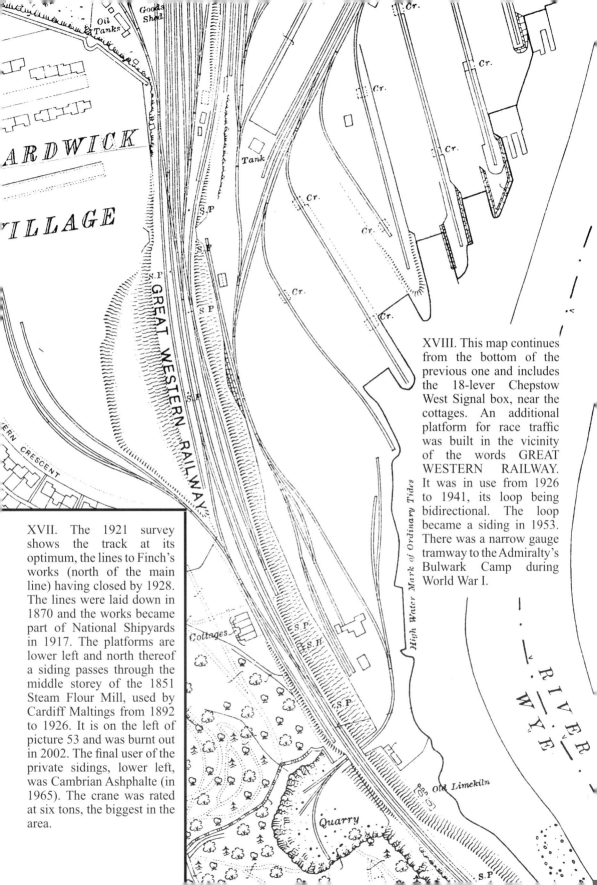

Oil Tanks

Goods Shed

Tank

ARDWICK

ILLAGE

Cr.

Cr.

Cr.

Cr.

Cr.

Cr.

Cr.

Cr.

S.P

S.P

S.P.

S.P

S.P

GREAT WESTERN RAILWAY

ERN CRESCENT

S.P

S.P.

S.P

Cottages

S.P

S.P

High Water Mark of Ordinary Tides

RIVER WYE

Old Limekiln

Quarry

S.P.

XVII. The 1921 survey shows the track at its optimum, the lines to Finch's works (north of the main line) having closed by 1928. The lines were laid down in 1870 and the works became part of National Shipyards in 1917. The platforms are lower left and north thereof a siding passes through the middle storey of the 1851 Steam Flour Mill, used by Cardiff Maltings from 1892 to 1926. It is on the left of picture 53 and was burnt out in 2002. The final user of the private sidings, lower left, was Cambrian Ashphalte (in 1965). The crane was rated at six tons, the biggest in the area.

XVIII. This map continues from the bottom of the previous one and includes the 18-lever Chepstow West Signal box, near the cottages. An additional platform for race traffic was built in the vicinity of the words GREAT WESTERN RAILWAY. It was in use from 1926 to 1941, its loop being bidirectional. The loop became a siding in 1953. There was a narrow gauge tramway to the Admiralty's Bulwark Camp during World War I.

56.   Brunel's chalet style roofing and later additions are included in this 1923 northward view. The platform on the right was termed a bay, although it was served by a loop. It was used by Monmouth trains from the north. The loop was taken out of use in 1927 when both platforms were extended eastwards. Wye Valley trains generally worked to and from Newport or Severn Tunnel Junction, giving a wider range of connections. (Stations UK)

57.   General freight traffic ceased on 7th April 1969 and the station was unstaffed from 6th October of that year. Here we witness an Intercity DMU passing the goods shed on its way to Cardiff on 24th April 1964. The shed was still standing in 2005. (M.A.N.Johnston)

58.   The exchange sidings are being shunted on 1st June 1964 and were still in place in 2005, although overgrown. The signal box had 55 levers and was used until 3rd March 1969. (R.G.Nelson/T.Walsh)

59.   A 1964 northeastward view in Fairfield Mabey's Shipyard includes two ex-Admiralty locomotives formerly used at Beachley Dock. The 0-4-0ST was built by Neilson & Co. in 1876 and became GER no. 0229. The 0-4-0WT was from Kerr Stuart in 1918. (M.A.N.Johnston)

Chepstow	1903	1913	1923	1933
Passenger tickets issued	66973	59395	67946	36836
Season tickets issued	*	*	784	946
Parcels forwarded	95960	93249	87626	80377
General goods forwarded (tons)	5743	6214	11741	7627
Coal and coke received (tons)	5521	3012	3015	1581
Other minerals received (tons)	3449	2656	3143	3146
General goods received (tons)	12781	12181	10511	16905
Trucks of livestock handled	701	930	549	314

(* not available.)

60. The sidings in the yard (right) of Fairfield Mabey were not used after 28th February 1985. No. 47348 has just crossed the rebuilt bridge on 27th April 1982, hauling empty coal wagons. (T.Heavyside)

61. The buildings were listed Grade II and renovated in 1982. They were in use as offices when photographed in September 1984. (D.Thompson)

62. The 07.35 Milford Haven to Birmingham New Street was recorded on 6th March 1995, passing the former goods shed and exchange sidings. The unit had passed the site of Thornwood signal box and the Admiralty sidings, in use during both world wars. (N.W.Sprinks)

PORTSKEWETT

XIX. The 1922 map at 6ins to 1 mile has the station on the right, together with the alignment of the route to the pier. On the left are dotted lines indicating the position of the Severn Tunnel, the

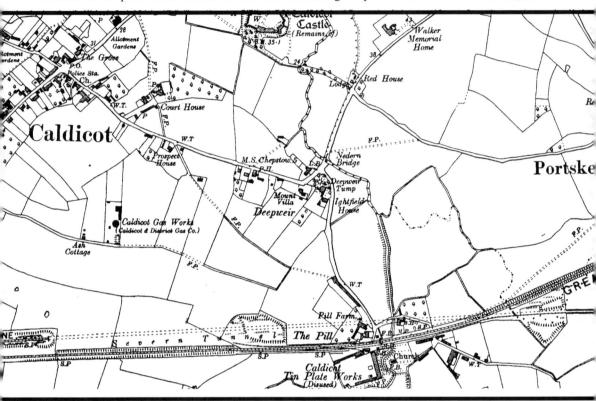

63. Portskewett Pier had a ferry service across the Severn to New Passage Pier, which is described in our *Branch Lines around Avonmouth*. The branch was open from 1st January 1864 to 1st December 1886, when the Severn Tunnel rendered it obsolete. In the background is the new Sudbrook Pump House. (C.G.Maggs coll.)

pumps of which are at Sudbrook, on the right page. The branch to the pumps and a shipyard runs above the tunnel.

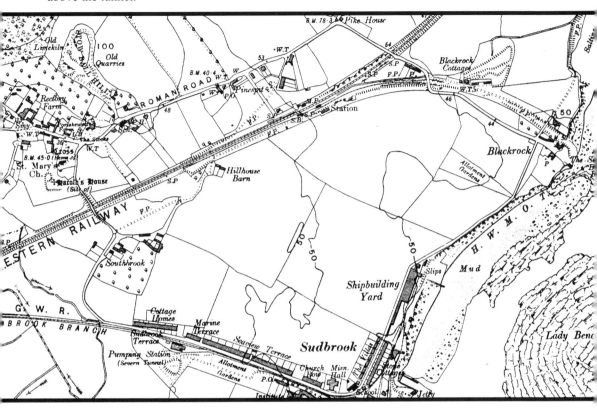

64. The station was repositioned in 1863, nearly ½ mile eastwards to the inconvenience of villagers. These buildings lasted until total closure of services on 2nd November 1964. There were six or seven men here in the 1930s. The signal box had 32 levers when closed on 1st May 1967. (Lens of Sutton coll.)

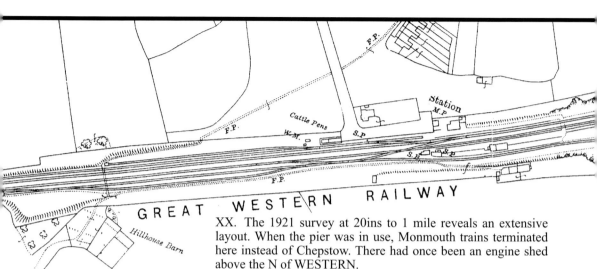

GREAT WESTERN RAILWAY

Hillhouse Barn

XX. The 1921 survey at 20ins to 1 mile reveals an extensive layout. When the pier was in use, Monmouth trains terminated here instead of Chepstow. There had once been an engine shed above the N of WESTERN.

Portskewett	1903	1913	1923	1933
Passenger tickets issued	20009	21372	27784	10226
Season tickets issued	*	*	279	138
Parcels forwarded	7032	7694	6789	1484
General goods forwarded (tons)	1808	2249	3004	1799
Coal and coke received (tons)	954	347	262	168
Other minerals received (tons)	426	1193	1610	282
General goods received (tons)	1666	1907	1702	406
Trucks of livestock handled	36	85	20	9
(* not available.)				

65. This view in the other direction is from about 1962, by which time the crossover was little used. The footbridge was built partly in front of the main building.
(Lens of Sutton coll.)

CALDICOT

66.   A train of coal for Sudbrook Pumps has reversed onto the down line before running forward onto the branch on 11th July 1959. The loco is no. 2292, a 2251 class 0-6-0. On the left is the private siding for Caldicot Works; on the right is the up refuge siding. The photo is from the 1927 59-lever Caldicot Junction signal box, which closed in 1969. (H.C.Casserley)

67.   Caldicot Halt opened on 12th September 1932, with timber platforms and Pagoda waiting huts. The 12.50 Gloucester to Cardiff departs on 9th July 2005 and is seen from the occupation crossing. The location is lower left on map XVI, above picture 51. (V.Mitchell)

CAERWENT

68.   The four-mile long branch was built to serve a Royal Naval Propellant Factory and opened for traffic on 2nd September 1943, although the builders used it from 30th November 1940. From 1969, it became RAF Caerwent, but was subsequently used by the US. The route has been added to map XVI, near picture 51, but not the sidings. The fire risk was so high in some areas that ropes and capstans were used for shunting, instead of locomotives. The site was in use by the MoD in 2005 for training purposes and the branch was in regular use, although weapon storage had ceased on the 1600 acre site in 1993. This view northwestwards is from March 1960. By 2002 parts of the site were leased for commercial use. EMUs and other coaches were brought here for storage and/or breaking up. (M.A.N.Johnston)

Great Western Railway
PORTSKEWETT JN. TO
NEW PASSAGE
THIRD   CLASS
Issued subject to the Conditions stated on the Co's. Time Bills.   (E.8)
New Passage   New Passage
562

2nd-SINGLE SINGLE-2nd
Severn Tunnel Junction to
SevernTunnelJn   SevernTunnelJn
CaldicotHt.   Caldicot Ht.
CALDICOT HALT
(W)   2d.   FARE   2d.   (W)
For conditions see over For conditions see over
5912   5912

SUDBROOK BRANCH

69.   This 1982 photograph was taken between the two level crossings, near the end of the branch. Beyond the gate, one line curves left towards the shipyard, which was served until 1919. No. 1 Engine House (centre) was built for six Cornish beam engines, but they ceased operation on 6th November 1961. A tunnel rescue train was kept here for many years, but a siding at Severn Tunnel Junction was dedicated for it subsequently. The Sudbrook branch was taken out of use in November 2004, apart from a short length for use as a siding. (D.H.Mitchell)

70.   The beam floor was recorded on 11th July 1959. The engines usually pumped 20m gallons daily, but could cope with 60m. For more tunnel details please see photos 77-87 in *Swindon to Newport*. (R.M.Casserley)

SEVERN TUNNEL JUNCTION

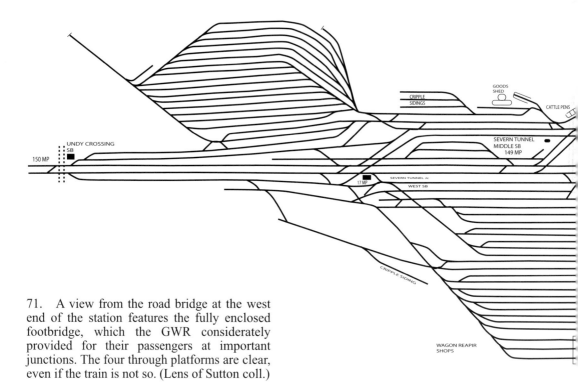

150 MP

UNDY CROSSING
SB

CRIPPLE
SIDINGS

GOODS
SHED

CATTLE PENS

SEVERN TUNNEL
MIDDLE SB
149 MP

17 MP

SEVERN TUNNEL Jc

WEST SB

CRIPPLE SIDING

WAGON REAPIR
SHOPS

71.   A view from the road bridge at the west end of the station features the fully enclosed footbridge, which the GWR considerably provided for their passengers at important junctions. The four through platforms are clear, even if the train is not so. (Lens of Sutton coll.)

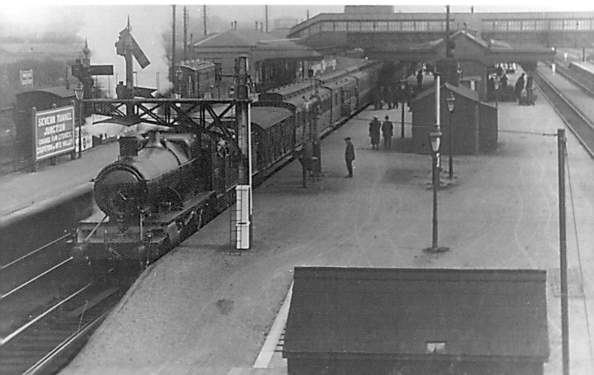

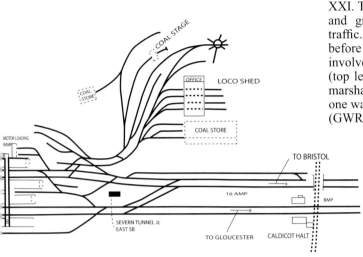

XXI. The station opened with the tunnel and gradually expanded in response to traffic. This 1931 diagram shows the layout before major expansion in 1939, which involved extension of the "Bristol Yard" (top left) westwards to form the up hump marshalling yard. The corresponding down one was created southeast of the platforms. (GWR Magazine)

72. An eastward panorama from 17th May 1953 includes the engine shed, beyond the water tower. The flat wagons coupled to a coach, on the left, formed the tunnel car carrying train. It is extensively illustrated in use in *Swindon to Newport* and was discontinued on 8th September 1966, when the first road bridge was opened. (R.G.Nelson/T.Walsh)

73.   Looking west on the same day, we witness 2-6-2T no. 6629 with an engineers train, while cattle wagons stand near the pens. The GWR canopy design avoided the need for stanchions in the platform. The right platform has not been used since 1968. (R.G.Nelson/T.Walsh)

74.   The shed was coded 86A by BR and is seen on 14th July 1958, with nos 5253 and 6672 on the left. The original 2-road shed, on the up side of the line near the station, came into use with the tunnel in 1886. It continued in use as a steam railmotor shed until 1927. The shed depicted opened in 1908; the cleaner extension followed in 1931. Both sheds were involved in providing banking engines for the tunnel, and later greatly involved with freight services starting from and terminating in the extensive yards. (H.C.Casserley)

75. A view westwards in 1965 includes the South Wales Pullman which is turning to take the up tunnel line in front of Middle Box, which had 85 levers. There was a payroll of 223 in 1937, this including traincrews. (S.V.Blencowe)

76. Station staffing ceased on 6th October 1969 and bus shelters had to suffice thereafter. The DMU is working the 16.00 Chepstow to Cardiff on 23rd September 1985, while no. 47223 passes over the hump, last used for marshalling purposes in 1981. Marshalling yards once stretched for 1½ miles alongside the main line. (D.H.Mitchell)

77. The yards closed in 1986 and some of the area was subjected to landscaping. No. 158872 passes the wilderness as it runs from Cardiff to Portsmouth Harbour on 26th June 2003. St. Mary's church was attended by many railway families, as they once outnumbered all others in this district. (M.Turvey)

UNDY HALT

78.   The halt was opened on 11th September 1933 and is seen in this westward view from about 1962. The outer lines came into use in September 1941 and were used for goods traffic. There was a lattice footbridge, spanning all four tracks, from which this photo was taken. The outer brick arches date from 1941. (Lens of Sutton coll.)

79.   The original Undy Crossing signalbox opened around 1913 with an 18-lever frame, later replaced by one of 30 levers. This box was replaced on quadrupling of the line in 1941 by one housing 47 levers, the latter closing in July 1960, together with the level crossing, its work being divided between Magor and Severn Tunnel Junction West signalboxes. Undy ground frame was provided at this time to control the entrance to eleven new reception sidings for the remodelled up hump yard. (J.G.S.Smith/Ted Hancock Books)

MAGOR

80.   The station opened with the line, although the population was less than 400. This eastward view is from about 1910 and the 1921 map is included in our *Swindon to Newport* album. The buildings were demolished in 1941. (Lens of Sutton coll.)

81.   An up freight was recorded on 1st December 1951 hauled by 2-8-2T no. 7213. As at Undy, the outer tracks and bridge arches date from 1941. St. Mary's Church is evident on the right, but the lattice footbridge is not clear. (P.Q.Treloar coll.)

82.   The 8.50am from Paddington on 11th July 1959 was headed by no. 5945 *Leckhampton Hall*. It is carrying the "Pembroke Coast Express" headboard. The six-ton crane can be seen in this and the previous photograph. (H.C.Casserley)

83.   The goods yard handled vast quantities of cement in the early 1960s, for the construction of the nearby steelworks. The goods yard closed on 26th July 1965 and the signal box followed on 1st December 1968. It had been extended by 12ft in 1941 to accommodate a new 47-lever frame; it had a panel in its final years. (Lens of Sutton coll.)

LLANWERN

XXII.   The map of 1921 shows little habitation nearby; there were under 300 villagers. The lower line on the right is the down refuge siding. West of the station was a single siding serving a goods shed.

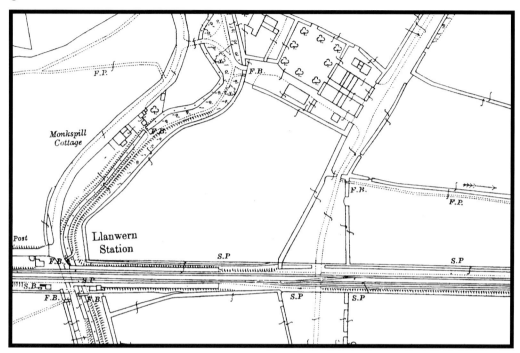

84.   This westward view includes the goods shed and loading gauge. The station opened with the line, but closed completely on 12th September 1960 in preparation for the building of the steelworks. The 40-lever signal box closed on 16th April 1961. The staff averaged nine in the 1930s. (Lens of Sutton coll.)

85. Following the quadrupling in 1941, two new platforms and a remote booking office were built. The station was closed for all traffic on 16th April 1961 and this is the scene a few years later. (Lens of Sutton coll.)

XXIII. The Spencer Steelworks issued these diagrams soon after it opened; it has had three owners. They have been Richard Thomas & Baldwin, British Steel Corporation and Corus. This is the eastern third of the site and curving top right from the main lines are two tracks, the up one of which passes over them on Bishton Flyover, which came into use on 17th April 1961. This end of the premises includes the rolling mills, which were still in use in 2005.

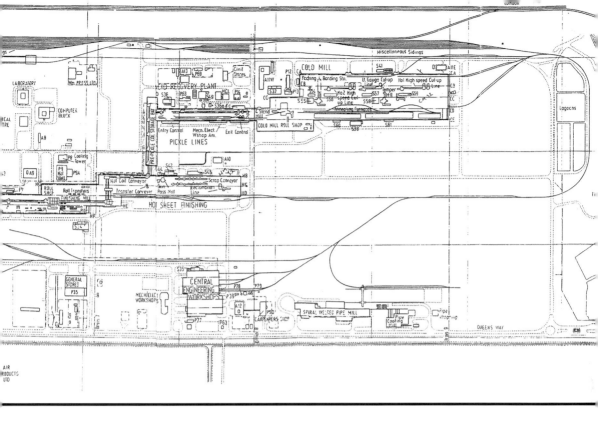

86.	The road bridge at the west end of the three mile long site was the only external location for photography. No. 08780 departs on a local trip with coal empties on 19th October 1979. (D.H.Mitchell)

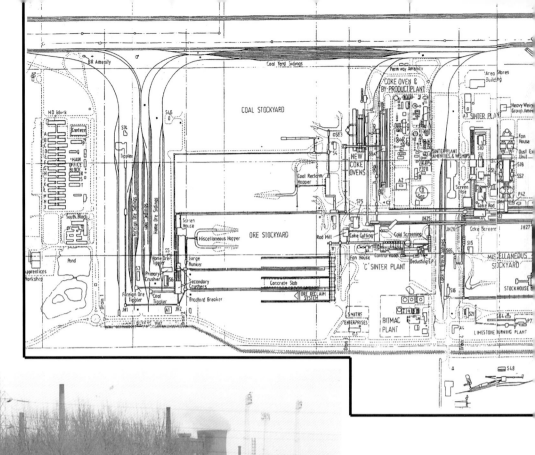

87. No. 60034 leaves with empties for Port Talbot, where imported coal would be loaded for the return trip. Steel making on the site ended in 2001 and much steel was subsequently imported through Port Talbot for rolling here. It also came through Newport Docks and Royal Portbury Docks on the other side of the Severn. The up and down relief lines are on the left. (B.Morrison)

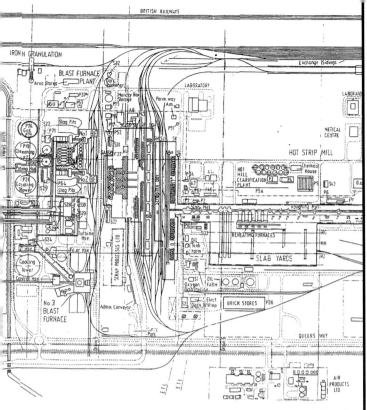

XXIV. Here is the centre part of the works, the right edge joining to the previous map. The plant had a capacity of two million tons of liquid steel per annum, which was increased to 3m in 1975. It was opened by H.M.Queen Elizabeth II on 26th October 1962 and a high of 9353 employees was reached in 1979.

88. No. 37704 heads a Merry-go-Round coal train in June 1995. Despatched by rail is a vast tonnage of steel in rolls for the motor industry and electrical goods manufacturers, but this mostly goes from the east end of the works. (Corus)

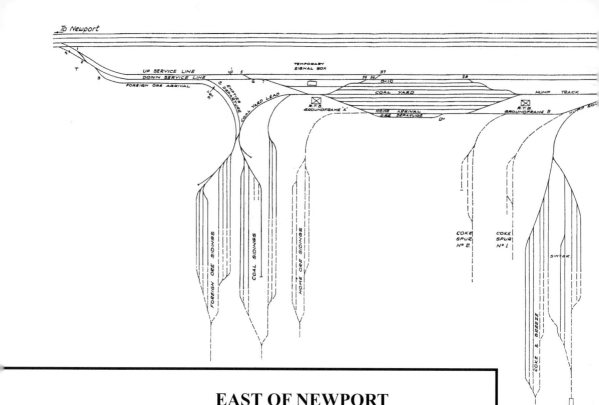

To Newport

UP SERVICE LINE
DOWN SERVICE LINE
FOREIGN ORE ARRIVAL

TEMPORARY
SIGNAL BOX

COAL YARD LEAD

EMPTIES ORE RETURN

COAL YARD

HUMP TRACK

GROUNDFRAME 'A'

HOME ARRIVAL
ORE DEPATURE

GROUNDFRAME B

HUMP SDG.

FOREIGN ORE SIDINGS

COAL SIDINGS

HOME ORE SIDINGS

COKE
SPUR
No 2

COKE
SPUR
No 1

SINTER

COKE & BREEZE

EAST OF NEWPORT

89. With steam rising from Llanwern Steelworks (in the background), no. 60035 *Florence Nightingale* approaches East Usk Junction with the 10.15 Round Oak-Margam Steel Service on 19th August 1995 . The line going off to the right is the freight only Uskmouth branch, opened in 1898 to service the Orb Steelworks, extended to the channel dry dock in 1901 and finally to the new Uskmouth Power Station in 1953. The branch has seen little traffic in recent years, though the power station took some deliveries of coal and lime in 2001-02. A regular working of imported coal from Newport Docks recommenced in January 2005. The 12 East Usk Junction sidings are behind the camera, as are the four Lliswery sidings and the 39-lever East Usk box, which works the semaphore on the right. (G.Gillham)

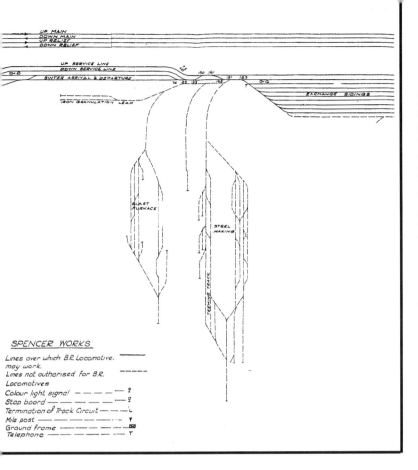

SPENCER WORKS

Lines over which B.R. Locomotive. may work.
Lines not authorised for B.R. Locomotives
Colour light signal — — — — — ●
Stop board — — — — — — ●
Termination of Track Circuit — — — ∟
Mile post — — — — — — ▼
Ground frame — — — — — ▣
Telephone — — — — — — T

XXV. The blast furnaces at the west end of the site are featured on this map, which is not continuous with the previous one. Much of this end of the plant has been demolished since 2001. There was a spiral welded pipe mill in use here between 1967 and 1975. A further 53 coke ovens, each over 63m high, were added in 1975, along with a blast furnace 11.2m in diameter.

XXVI. The 1905 diagram has our route from right to bottom and shows the present station as "High Street", a name it never carried officially. The darkest line is that of the Alexandra Dock & Railway, which became part of the GWR in 1922. The passenger termini at Dock Street and Mill Street closed in the 1880s. (Railway Clearing House)

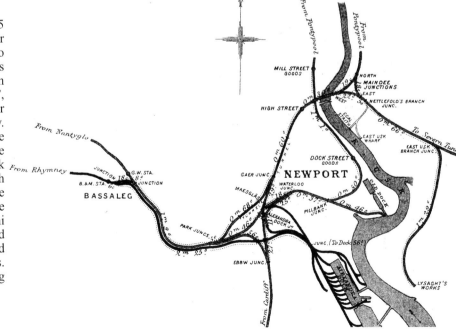

NEWPORT

90. The bridge over the River Usk east of the station was built of timber and severely damaged by fire on 7th June 1848, before it had carried a passenger. One span was immediately replaced by wrought iron and the others followed in 1886. (C.G.Maggs coll.)

→

XXVII. The 1st edition of 1880 includes two footbridges, the northern one being for public use. Of the sheds on the left, the upper one was for carriages and the lower one for engines, this closing in 1915. Some of the upper sidings were still used for berthing locomotives in 2005, those of EW&S. They are known as Godfrey Road Sidings. The tunnel at the bottom is in fact two: Old Tunnel (742yds) is on the right, while on the left is New Tunnel of 1912 (762yds).

91. This westward panorama was recorded from the footbridge and has the goods shed on the left, the engine shed being in the distance. The broad gauge was converted to standard in 1872. (C.G.Maggs coll.)

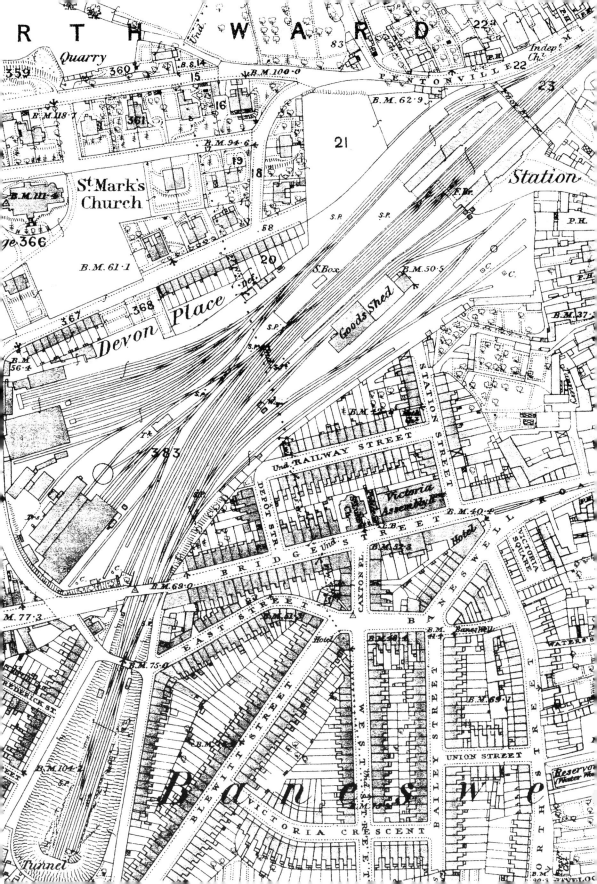

92. Period atmosphere is created by this record of class 770 0-6-0ST no. 770 taking water on 22nd April 1905. The staff rose from 187 in 1903 to 298 in 1923; these figures exclude those involved with goods traffic. (K.Nunn/LCGB)

**Other views of this station can be found in *Brecon to Newport*
and *Swindon to Newport*.**

93. Approaching the platforms from the west on 2nd September 1957 is 2-8-0T no. 4282; coal dust and smoke accumulated in this cutting. On the right is the 144-lever West Box, which had an advanced electrical route setting system, as did East Box. Both closed on 10th December 1962. (M.Dart)

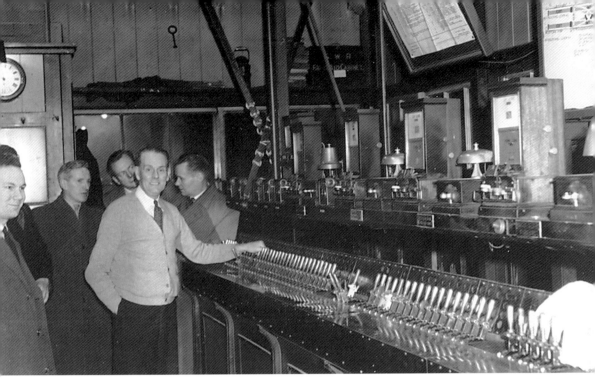

94.   The system was tried at Winchester Chesil in 1923-33 and installed at Newport in 1927. The unusual miniature levers caused some amusement during a visit on 14th January 1961. All signals and points were electrically operated. (M.H.Walshaw)

95.   An undated view features 4-6-0 no. 75022 with a down stopping train. Devoid of wires, levers and balance weights, the signals look tidy. The lower arms, together with two under the canopy, show CO, which indicates "Calling On" or proceed with caution towards a line already occupied by a train or standing vehicles. (J.Moss/R.S.Carpenter)

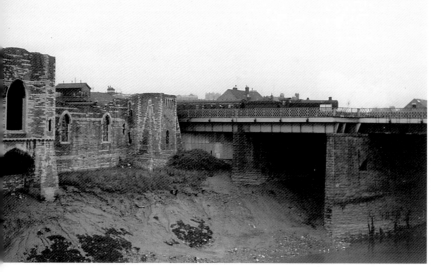

96. East Box had 96 miniature levers and is on the left of this view of a "Hall" class 4-6-0 departing east. The tidal differential in South Wales can be as much as 40ft, creating ugly estuaries, but good defensive positions for the castles. (R.Holmes)

97. The rebuilding of the station lasted from 1923 to 1930 and the south facade was photographed in May 1986. It still has the main entrance, although the nearest platform is used by few passenger trains. (C.G.Maggs)

98. Seen on 21st November 2003 is the back of the building together with the footbridge. No. 66231 is hauling a Railtrack engineers train. The 1962 panel box is obscured by the rear of the train. (M.Dart)

99.   No. 47507 emerges from New Tunnel on 26th March 1976 and approaches Gaer Junction. The nearest tracks were termed "Main" and the others "Relief". Note the difference in tunnel dimensions. (T.Heavyside)

100. Seen in the opposite direction on the same day is no. 47181 with an up express. Rising on the right is the route to Bassaleg and the Western Valleys. It was subsequently singled and was still used by stone trains from Machen in the next century. Gaer Tunnel is on the right. (T.Heavyside)

101. The massive Ebbw Junction engine shed opened on 17th July 1915. The repair shop had nine roads accessed by this traverser. The electric supply can be seen above each doorway and the collector pole is near the dome of no. 9746. The BR shed code was 86A; closure was in October 1965. (R.S.Carpenter)

102. Ebbw Junction Diesel Depot was opened in 1966 and photographed on 25th September 1980. The apron lower right was adjacent to the washing plant. The pole on the right of this picture is on the left of the next one. (D.H.Mitchell)

103. Nos.37307,37308 and 37303 haul empty iron ore wagons from Llanwern to Margam on the down relief road on 26th March 1976. The Cardiff Curve to Ebbw Junction is on the left. In the background is the bridge built for the Alexandra Dock & Railway. On the right are some of the 20 lines of the Alexandra Dock Junction Marshalling Yard. (T.Heavyside)

MARSHFIELD

XXVIII. The 1922 map at 6ins to 1 mile reveals the small size of the nearby communities and their proximity to the station. Marshfield had a population of 581 in 1901. There were only three trains each way on weekdays in 1869. There was only one more when it closed.

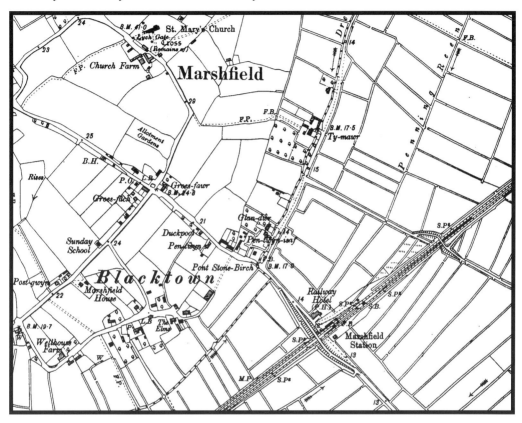

104. A panorama from the footbridge in 1935 includes the relief lines, which were completed in stages in 1896-98. The employees numbered 13 to 14 in the 1930s. The station opened with the line and closed to passengers on 10th August 1959.
(Stations UK)

105. Looking east from the footbridge, we gain a glimpse of the goods yard, which closed on 4th January 1965. The 39-lever signal box was in use from 1897 to 1963. Speeding west is no. 5093 *Upton Castle*; it is passing a row of milk tankers. Five were despatched to London each day for many years. (C.S.Cann/ P.Q.Treloar coll.)

106. The down platform was removed after closure, but the up side remained intact, together with its sliding iron gate. The photo is from about 1962. (Lens of Sutton coll.)

Marshfield	1903	1913	1923	1933
Passenger tickets issued	23504	27640	18109	11626
Season tickets issued	*	*	209	326
Parcels forwarded	2607	4200	4068	2691
General goods forwarded (tons)	407	793	1589	720
Coal and coke received (tons)	759	4077	11548	148
Other minerals received (tons)	2544	4077	11548	148
General goods received (tons)	268	718	1453	473
Trucks of livestock handled	140	54	292	148

(* not available.)

EAST OF CARDIFF

107. Passing Pengam Down Yard on the down main line is 4-6-2 no. 70017 *Arrow*. The date was not recorded, but the yard closed on 7th November 1966 and was converted to a Freightliner terminal. There were 15 such Britannia class locos allocated to Cardiff (Canton) in 1957. (C.E.Cann/ P.Q.Treloar coll.)

108. Pengam Freightliner facilities came into use in June 1967 and were photographed on 9th July 1998 with nos 47301 and 47367 about to leave for Coatbridge at 18.20. The work of the depot was transferred to a new terminal at Wentloog, one mile to the east, on 13th February 2001. The new A4232 is in the background. (D.H.Mitchell)

109. From the other side of the bridge, we witness the passage of an HST working the 15.35
Swansea to Paddington service on 23rd October 1982. The lines on the left form the Roath Docks
branch which (since 1925) joined the former Taff Vale line (1888-1968), which crossed the bridge
in the background. The branch served Tidal Sidings, Roath Dock, Queen Alexandra Docks, Gulf
Oil Terminal and Allied Steel & Wire Ltd. On the right is Roath Yard. (T.Heavyside)

110. This indifferent view features Cardiff Railway 0-6-0ST no. 14 on 27th July 1922. We are looking west from the footbridge shown in the top right corner of the left page of map XXIX. The flour mill is in the background. (R.S.Carpenter coll.)

111. This westward panorama is from the Rhymney Railway bridge which was not used after December 1964. Two class 56s are working from Port Talbot to Llanwern in about 1980. On the right is the former GWR Newtown Goods Depot, used by National Carriers after 1972. On the left is Tyndall Fields Yard, the sidings of which were lifted in 1983. The area is top right on the next page. (N.W.Sprinks)

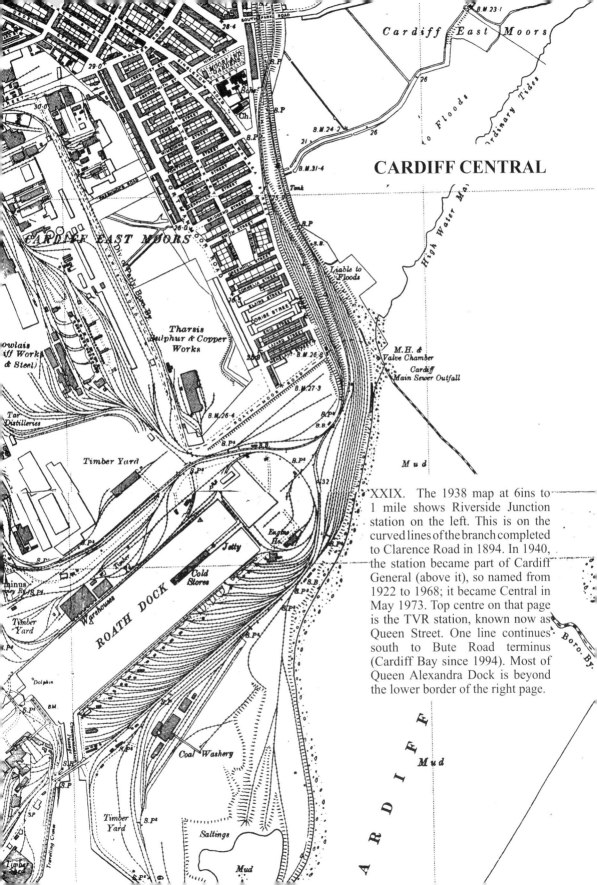

CARDIFF CENTRAL

XXIX. The 1938 map at 6ins to 1 mile shows Riverside Junction station on the left. This is on the curved lines of the branch completed to Clarence Road in 1894. In 1940, the station became part of Cardiff General (above it), so named from 1922 to 1968; it became Central in May 1973. Top centre on that page is the TVR station, known now as Queen Street. One line continues south to Bute Road terminus (Cardiff Bay since 1994). Most of Queen Alexandra Dock is beyond the lower border of the right page.

112. The premises were altered and enlarged in 1876-77 following the abandonment of broad gauge in the area. This is the east end in about 1904, after new platforms (left) had been provided for the TVR in 1896. There is a bay platform on the right and two through lines in the centre. The viaduct for trains to Queen Street came into use in 1897. (Lens of Sutton coll.)

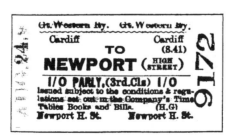

113. Further rebuilding in 1933-34 resulted in seven through platforms, plus a bay at the west end (numbered 5) and three through lines. On "Down Middle" on 6th July 1947 is 2-8-0T no. 4296 and the bay is on the right. (H.C.Casserley)

114. Approaching platform 8 on its way to Clarence Road on 5th May 1951 is 2-6-2T no. 4177. It will have started its journey in the Barry area. The disc BA indicates "Barry Passenger Duty A". (H.C.Casserley)

115. This bridge is immediately east of the station and passing over it with a local train from Newport on 25th July 1953 is no. 7910 *Hown Hall*. The bridge spanned the Glamorganshire Canal and is seen from the Central Hotel. (P.Glenn/R.S.Carpenter)

116. Both middle roads were occupied briefly on 12th July 1958 as no. 5204 hauled a load of coal west, probably to Barry Docks and no. 73127 waits for the signals. The lines to Queen Street are on the right. (G.Adams/M.J.Stretton)

117. The British and Commonwealth Games in 1958 was justification for this elaborate decoration. For more information about the wires, see *Cardiff Trolleybuses* (Middleton Press 2005). (G.Adams/M.J.Stretton)

118. The 1934 booking hall was lined with green and black marble; it was modernised in 1982 and was photographed in September 1984. There was and is a smaller entrance on the south side. (D.Thompson)

Other views of this station can be found in our *Branch Lines around Barry*.

119. The 11.55 all stations to Chepstow waits at platform 2 on 24th October 1989. There were three further such departures on weekdays at that period. (M.J.Stretton)

120. Diesel admirers were out in force on 15th June 2002 for the first visit of a class 52 for 25 years. It was D1015 *Western Champion*. We apologise for not including many other popular classes in this volume, but at least we have visited many interesting locations. (P.G.Barnes)

MP Middleton Press

EVOLVING THE ULTIMATE RAIL ENCYCLOPEDIA

Easebourne Lane, Midhurst, West Sussex.
GU29 9AZ   Tel:01730 813169

www.middletonpress.co.uk   email:info@middletonpress.co.uk
A-0 906520   B-1 873793   C-1 901706   D-1 904474

OOP Out of Print at time of printing - Please check current availability **BROCHURE AVAILABLE SHOWING NEW TITLES**